Bunyan and Banjoes

Michigan Songs & Stories

by Kitty Donohoe
& Pasqua Cekola Warstler

illustrated by
Pasqua Cekola Warstler

Thunder Bay Press

Our aim in putting together *Bunyan and Banjoes* has been to create a "user friendly" book for teachers, parents and children that celebrates the uniqueness of Michigan.

We encourage you to make the projects, cook the recipes, and share the songs and stories at home and school, savoring the special flavor of the "mitten state."

We'd like to thank those who helped us along the way with advice, information and suggestions.

Mike Ackles
Tom Ackles
Bement Public Library
Becky Larner
Joseph and Becky LaToff
Gene and Carol Livingston
Michigan Commission of Indian Affairs
John and Catherine Rumbaugh
Eliot Singer
Joy Sytsma
Bill Tennant
Tom Warstler
Jim Wieber
Diantha Witteveen

Special thanks go to Diana Grinwis and Jim Pratl
and most especially to
our own Michigan Kids
Jesse, Page, Callie, Bailey, Whitney, Elspeth, and Kirsten

"Red Iron Ore," "Louie Sands and Jim McGee" are public domain.

The melodies to "Michigan Gals," "Rivers," and "Michigan ABC" are public domain.

All other songs are by Kitty Donohoe and are the property of
Roheen Music, P.O. Box 1813, East Lansing, Michigan 48826-1813

Contents
Song Index

Activities

Maple syrup is said to have been a staple food of the Indians who are credited with introducing it to Michigan's early settlers. The scarcity of white sugar on the frontier helped maple sweetening become very popular with early Michiganders, and we still make syrup almost like our ancestors did many years ago. In late winter or early spring when the sap begins to rise in the trees, a spout (or spile) is inserted into a small hole drilled into the trunk of a sugar maple tree. A bucket is hung below the spout to catch the sap; and when the buckets are full, they are taken to a special building called a "sugar house" or "sugar shack." Some maple sugar farms have started using plastic tubing instead of spiles to collect the sap so that it runs directly from the trees into a large collection vat. Once in the sugar house, the sap is boiled until most of the water evaporates leaving a thick maple syrup. It takes about 40 gallons of maple sap to get 1 gallon of maple syrup!

When the Indians wanted to make maple syrup, they would put the sap in a hollow log and place hot rocks from the fire into the log, replacing the cooling rocks with more hot ones. As you can imagine, it took a long time to turn the sap into syrup.

Michigan is the third largest producer of maple syrup in the country.

This is an easy recipe for a delicious, mapley snack. You could give some to your babysitter (oops! kidwatcher) the next time he or she comes over.

The ingredient amounts are approximate. Adjust accordingly.

MAPLE ROASTED NUTS

½ cup maple syrup
4 cups raw peanuts

Stove Method: In a large saucepan combine the peanuts and syrup and cook on medium heat, stirring every few minutes until the peanuts are thoroughly coated with the syrup. This will take about 15 minutes. Then spread the peanuts on a greased cookie sheet, salt lightly and roast in a warm oven (200-250 degrees) for 40 minutes to an hour.

Microwave Method: Combine peanuts and syrup in a microwave-safe bowl and zap on high for about 15 minutes, stirring at 5 minute intervals until nuts are coated with syrup. Roast in regular oven as above.

SNOW WONDER

For a special winter treat, heat a cup of syrup to about 235 degrees—a candy thermometer would help—and without stirring, pour immediately on a patch of clean snow to make designs or initials. When the syrup cools in a few minutes, you'll have a chewy maple syrup candy!

Maple Syrup

Verse

When the win-ter winds are blow-in a-way and warm spring sun-shine's here to stay,

sap starts creep-in' up the tree to make a treat for you and me and it

Chorus (spoken)

tastes *so good!* *How good?* *So good!* *Real good?* *So good!* It's ma- ple syr- up and it

tastes *so good! How* *good? So good! Real* *good? So good!* It's ma- ple syr- up   First you

First you make a hole in the side of the tree
Sometimes two and sometimes three
And in that hole you place a spout
Where the sap comes slowly trickling out
And it tastes. . .

You put it in a pan that's wide and flat
And take it down to the sugar shack
Boil it slowly over the heat
Til it comes out thick and sticky and sweet
And it tastes. . .

You can eat it on pancakes, waffles, too
Biscuits, ice cream, from a spoon
In winter time wherever you are
You can pour a little sunshine from a jar
And it tastes. . .

Indian Lore

About 600 years ago the Ojibwa was one huge Indian tribe, centered on the Atlantic coast of Canada north of the St. Lawrence River. Gradually a large segment of that tribe moved westward, stopping for lengths of time at the St. Lawrence River, Lake Huron, and what is now the town of Sault Ste. Marie, Michigan. At about this time, the big tribe split into three smaller ones: the Potawatomi, or "those-who-make-or-keep-a-fire"; the Ottawa, or "traders"; and the Ojibwas, now called Chippewa, meaning "to-toast-till-puckered-up." Smaller tribes in Michigan included the Huron, Miami, Menominee, and the Wyandotte. Many counties and rivers in Michigan still have their original Indian names such as Leelenau, Kalamazoo, Keweenaw, Ontonagon, Escanaba, and Manistee.

Henry Rowe Schoolcraft was born in 1793 in a small village in New York. He was always interested in writing and in learning new things. Because of his interest in American Indians, he was named the Indian Agent for the Upper Great Lakes in 1822. His headquarters were in Sault Ste. Marie. When he first arrived, he stayed with a man named John Johnston and his wife, Susan. Susan was the daughter of a famous Chippewa chief, Waub Ojeeg, a reknowned storyteller. Henry married John and Susan's daughter, Jane, and with the help of Jane, her brother, George, and their mother, he spent many years collecting and translating the legends of North American Indians. This tale was taken from his book of those stories, *The Hiawatha Legends*, and is from the Ottawa.

PEETA KWAY, OR THE FOAM WOMAN

Many years ago there lived on the shores of Lake Michigan, on the sand mountains called "Sleeping Bear," a woman who had a beautiful young daughter. This girl was so pretty that her mother was afraid that someone would steal her, so she kept her in a box that floated out on the lake. The box was tied to a stake on the shore with a string and every morning the mother would pull in the box, feed her daughter and comb her lovely black hair, then put her back in the box and float it out on the lake again.

One morning a handsome young man was passing by when the woman was combing her daughter's hair, and he was struck by the girl's beauty. He went home to discuss his feelings with his uncle and to ask advice on winning the girl's hand in marriage. The uncle, who was a very powerful magician, told his nephew to return to the woman's lodge (house) and to sit quietly beside her. Through his thoughts the woman would know what the young man wanted, and likewise, he would know her thoughts. The youth did as he was told. While sitting beside the older woman he thought, "Please give me your daughter in marriage." The mother thought to herself, "My daughter! Absolutely not! You're not good enough for her."

The young man returned home and told his uncle what had happened. The uncle was angry and consulted with the spirits of the lake who decided to teach the mother a lesson for her excessive pride. They brewed up a terrible storm on the lake with wind and rain and waves so high that the string on the box broke and the girl floated away. The box sailed all the way through the Straits and into Lake Huron where it struck against the sandy shores of that lake. The box landed near the lodge of an old spirit, Ishkwon Daimeka, who opened the box, rescued the beautiful girl and married her.

When the mother discovered her daughter was gone, she cried and grieved endlessly. After a few years the spirits took pity on the woman and created another huge storm that tossed and raged worse than the first. As soon as the storm began, the girl leaped into the box and was carried all the way back to the shores by her mother's lodge. The woman found her daughter and was overjoyed to have her back, even though she had lost most of her beauty. The mother immediately sent a message to the young man to offer her daughter in marriage, but he was no longer interested and refused the offer.

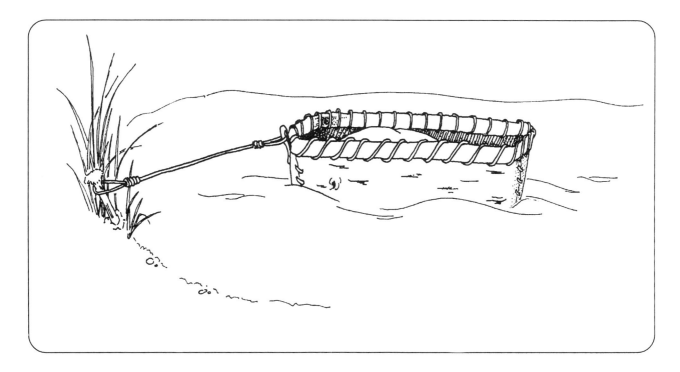

Meanwhile, the storm that had carried the girl home again had torn off a large part of the shore of Lake Huron, including the lodge of Ishkwon Daimeka. As the shoreline was being swept away, many smaller fragments broke off and were left behind becoming the beautiful islands we see in the Detroit and St. Clair Rivers.

Here are some Indian recipes given to us by the Michigan Commission on Indian Affairs.

CORN CHOWDER

½ pound salt pork, diced
1 onion, peeled and chopped
½ green pepper, cored and chopped
1 potato, peeled and diced
2 tablespoons butter

½ teaspoon salt
1/8 teaspoon black pepper
2 (10 oz.) pkgs. frozen corn
3 tablespoons parsley
2½ cups milk or light cream

Render the salt pork slowly in a large, heavy skillet. Add the onion, green pepper, potato, and butter. Sauté until the potato is tender, about 20 minutes. Add the salt, black pepper, and corn. Heat, stirring, until the corn has thawed. Stir in parsley and milk or cream and simmer gently, stirring until heated through. Do not boil. Serve at once.

AMERICAN INDIAN CORN BREAD

¼ cup butter, softened
1 cup yellow cornmeal
1½ cups unsifted all-purpose flour
½ cup sugar
2 eggs
1 cup canned pumpkin

¼ cup milk
3 teaspoons baking powder
1 teaspoon salt
1 cup blueberries, drained
½ cup chopped walnuts

Beat together butter, sugar, and eggs until smooth. Add pumpkin, milk, and cornmeal and continue to beat until well blended. Sift together flour, baking powder, and salt. Using a wooden spoon, stir flour mixture into pumpkin mixture just until ingredients are combined. Fold in blueberries and walnuts. Spoon batter into a lightly greased 9 x 5 x 2 inch loaf pan. Bake at 350 degrees for about one hour or until bread tests done.

RHUBARB PUDDING
(SHEE-WEE-BUG)

2 cups diced rhubarb
1 cup plus 2 tablespoons flour
1 teaspoon grated orange rind
2/3 cup honey
2 tablespoons sugar

½ teaspoon salt
½ teaspoon baking powder
¼ cup shortening
1 egg, slightly beaten
¼ cup milk

Mix rhubarb with the 2 tablespoons flour, orange rind, honey and some cinnamon to taste. Put in an 8 inch square pan. Mix remaining flour, sugar, salt, and baking powder. Cut in shortening. Stir together the egg and milk and add to the flour mixture. Spread on rhubarb and bake for 40 minutes at 350 degrees. Cool and turn upside down on a serving plate.

INDIAN FRY BREAD

4 cups flour
4 teaspoons baking powder
1 teaspoon salt

¼ cup shortening
¾ cup milk
fat for frying

Mix first 3 ingredients. Cut in shortening and add enough milk to make a soft dough. Roll out on a floured board, cut in pieces. Fry in hot fat, turning once until golden brown. Yields about 32 pieces.

The Fur Trade

By the mid-1600s the fur trade in Michigan was booming due to the popularity in Europe of fur-trimmed clothing. Trappers collected the furs of otter, martin, raccoon, mink, muskrat and weasel, but the beaver fur was by far the most sought after when the broad-brimmed beaver hat became all the rage. King Louis XIV of France was anxious to get a foothold on this new enterprise and encouraged young men to come to the new world. Soon there were hundreds of French and French-Canadian trappers in Michigan hoping to get rich exporting furs.

The most colorful of these men were the voyageurs, or boatmen, who could paddle their canoes as far as 100 miles in a day, often singing together to relieve the tedium. Distance on the rivers was measured in "smokes" or "pipes" instead of miles by the voyageurs because they would rest from their furious paddling every two or three miles for a quick puff on their pipes.

Because of their singing and their colorful clothes (they wore trousers, high leather leggings, shirts belted with bright, gaudy sashes and red caps struck with a feather) they had the reputation of being carefree and unambitious. They were actually very hard workers and soon discovered that the Indians would give them furs for items the voyageurs could supply from the outside world such as brass kettles, muskets, wrought-iron axeheads and brandy.

Carrying trade goods for the Indians and returning with loads of furs was a very hard task for the voyageurs. When they had to carry items from one body of water to another, called "portaging," the men would tie the goods in 90-pound bundles and strap two of these packs on their backs with a "tumpline," a moosehide strap that went across their foreheads and down their backs. With their canoes and bundles they would then hike through forests, swamps and underbrush to the next body of water where they would resume their canoeing.

Voyageurs

In our caps of apple red, sashes of bright yellows
We're as handsome as the birds sitting in the trees
Even when we're working hard we are merry fellows
When we have a song to sing with many harmonies
Chorus

Even in the cold and rain we don't worry do we?
We just laugh and turn our backs and sing another song
Trapping beaver and muskrat for the good King Louie
Or trading with the Indians as we go along
Chorus

Now our home is Michigan, we don't want another
We're content to stay right here with one regret
How we miss the cooking of our Auntie and our Mother
We would love a fat croissant and an omelette!
Chorus

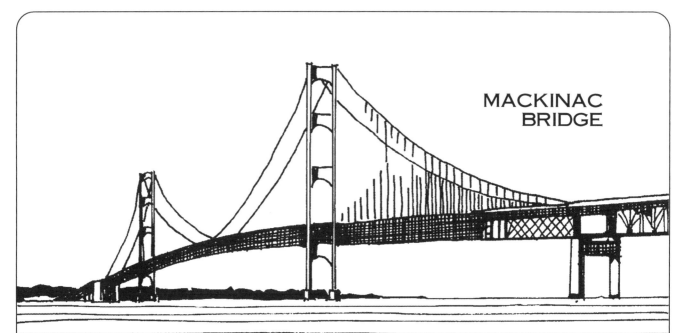

MACKINAC BRIDGE

Mackinac Island is famous for its fudge shops. Half the fun of "fudging" is watching the candymakers work energetically with the fudge as it cools on a marble slab. This recipe isn't nearly as athletic, but it's easy to make and tastes wonderful. Little cooks will need some help.

The Mackinac Bridge is a magnificent achievement. It stretches from St. Ignace in the Upper Peninsula to Mackinaw City in the Lower Peninsula. The towers rise 552 feet into the air. Work on the bridge began in the spring of 1954 and was completed in November, 1957. The span enables a steady flow of traffic to cross the Straits. A trip that used to take many hours by ferry can now be accomplished in just a few minutes.

LANDLUBBER'S FUDGE

1½ cups sugar	1 (7 oz) jar marshmallow creme
¼ cup margarine	12 oz pkg. chocolate chips
2/3 cup evaporated milk	1 teaspoon vanilla
¼ teaspoon salt	1 cup chopped nuts (optional)

Combine sugar, margarine, milk, salt, and marshmallow creme in a large saucepan. Bring to a boil over moderate heat and continue boiling for 5 minutes, stirring constantly to prevent scorching. Remove from heat and add remaining ingredients, stirring to melt the chocolate chips. Pour into a buttered 8-inch square pan and cool.

The Mackinac Bridge

Chorus

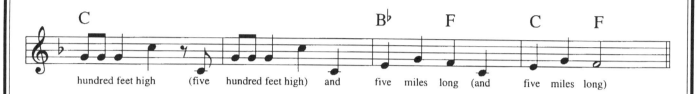

Oh, the Mack-i-naw Bridge (oh, the Mack-i-nac Bridge) she's a might-y fine bridge (she's a might-y fine bridge) five

hundred feet high (five hundred feet high) and five miles long (and five miles long)

Verse

in the Straits of Mack- i- nac there's a- bout as much wa-ter as you ev- er saw and the

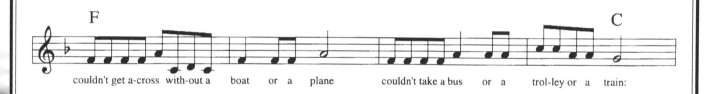

folks who lived there tried and tried but they couldn't get a-cross to the oth- er side,

couldn't get a-cross with-out a boat or a plane couldn't take a bus or a trol-ley or a train:

couldn't swim a-cross it was as cold as a fridge! so they thought they bet-ter build them- selves a bridge, Oh, the

So in nineteen hundred and fifty-four they started linking shore to shore
From Mackinaw City to St. Ignace town, and the men on the top didn't dare look down!
In 'fifty-seven the work was through, and there she was all shiny and new
So they had a big party and they called out loud "She's the Mackinac Bridge and we are proud!"

Chorus

Mining

Michigan's many mineral resources have played an important part in developing our state. As well as having significant amounts of gypsum, limestone, sand, gravel and coal, we have one of the largest salt deposits in the world. In fact, beneath the streets of Detroit there is a huge mine operated by the International Salt Company that still runs full-time. Most of the salt from the mine is used as rock salt, industrial salt and brine solutions, with only about 2 percent being used for table salt. The minerals that really brought industry to Michigan, however, were copper and iron ore. At the same time that the lumber boom was settling the Lower Peninsula in the 1840s, huge deposits of copper and iron ore were being discovered in the western Upper Peninsula.

COPPER—The area we call the "Copper Country" centers around the Keweenaw Peninsula where towns like Houghton and Calumet were born and thrived on the copper trade, becoming home to thousands of Swedes, Norwegians and Finns who came to work in the mines and established churches, schools, colleges and newspapers. From 1847 to 1887, Michigan produced more copper than any other state, almost 90% of the national total output.

IRON ORE—At the same time that copper was discovered in the Upper Peninsula, veins of iron ore were found in the western part of the peninsula below the Copper Country. Michigan has three enormous iron ranges: the Marquette Range, the Menominee Range and the Gogebic Range. When railroads were built in the wilderness to carry the ore, it became feasible to mine these ranges. Another method of transporting ore was by boat, which helped the Great Lakes shipping trade to flourish during the mining years. Huge loads of ore were shipped from the Upper Peninsula to other large Midwestern ports or to the East where it went to steel mills and foundries. By the early 1900s, however, the mines began to be exhausted, and the steady decline in production turned some once bustling mining towns into ghost towns. Some that still stand are Fayette, Central, Victoria, Michigamme, and East Norway.

Soo Locks

St. Marys River by Sault Ste. Marie is a natural waterway between Lake Superior and Lake Huron and would be the obvious way to ship iron ore from the Upper Peninsula to the East. There's one problem: Lake Superior is 21 feet higher than Lake Huron, and the St. Marys River has a series of "rapids" or quick drops of water that would break up any boat that tried to pass through. For years men tried to get ships through the St. Marys anyway, sometimes pushing them around the rapids on rollers.

Finally in 1853 the river was deepened into a canal, and a series of chambers or "locks" was built over the rapids to enable ships to pass safely through. The Soo Locks work like this: a ship traveling from Lake Superior to Lake Huron floats into a huge box or lock, whose water level has been filled to match that of Lake Superior. The gates are then closed behind the ship which now waits in the lock for the water to be released back out. The valves near the bottom of the chamber allow enough water to flow out until the water level in the lock matches that of Lake Huron. Now the downstream gates are opened, and it is safe for the ship to continue. The process is reversed for westbound ships.

Red Iron Ore

A Traditional Great Lakes Song

Come all you bold sail-ors that fol-low the Lakes, on an i-ron ore ves-sel your

liv-ing to make. I shipped in Chi-ca-go, bid a-dieu to the shore, bound a-

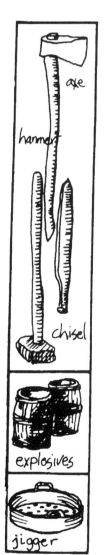

way for Es-ca-na-ba for red i-ron ore, der-ry down, down, down, der-ry, down.

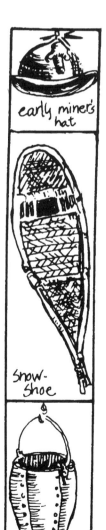

In the month of September on the seventeenth day
Two dollars and a quarter was all they would pay
And on Monday morning a trip we did take
On a ship called the *Roberts* sailing out in the lake
Derry down, down, down derry down

The packet she howled 'cross the mouth of Green Bay
And before her cut water she threw the white spray
She rounded out Sand Point and her anchor let go
We furled in the canvas and the watch went below
Derry down, down, down derry down

Next morning we hove alongside the *Exile*
We soon made her fast to that iron ore pile
They lowered the chutes which soon started to roar
They're fillin' the ship with that red iron ore
Derry down, down, down derry down

Some sailors took shovels and others took spades
And some took to sluicing each man to his trade
We looked like red devils, our backs they got sore
We cursed Escanaba and that red iron ore
Derry down, down, down derry down

The dust got so thick you could scarce see your nose
It got in your eyes and it got in your clothes
We loaded the *Roberts* till she couldn't hold more
Right up to the gunnels with the red iron ore
Derry down, down, down derry down

We sailed her to Cleveland, made fast stem and stern
And with our companions we'll spin a big yarn
Here's a health to the *Roberts*, she's strong and she's true
Here's a health to the bold boys who make up her crew
Derry down, down, down derry down

Help us get our ore from the Upper Peninsula mines to the manufacturing plants downstate. Follow the maze path without crossing over lines and find your way to the loading dock at Marquette, through the Soo Locks and down through Lake Huron. Make sure to stop at the smelting plant at River Rouge before you reach Detroit.

The Pasty

During the 1840s miners from Cornwall, England came to the Upper Peninsula to help fill a shortage of manpower. Along with highly-developed mining skills, the Cornishmen brought with them a meat pie called a "pasty" to our state that quickly became an established food in the Upper Peninsula.

Some say the word "pasty" comes from "past day," meaning yesterday's meal of meat and vegetables which was folded into a crust for lunch the next day. The miners would carry their hot pasties to work against their chests to keep warm on frigid winter mornings and at noon would reheat the pies over their miner's lamps.

CORNISH PASTIES

Crust

4 cups flour	1½ cups vegetable shortening
2 teaspoons salt	1 cup ice water

In large bowl mix flour with salt. Cut in shortening with two butter knives or fingers until particles are about the size of small peas. Gradually add water, tossing with flour until dough forms into a ball. Cover with plastic wrap and keep in refrigerator while making filling.

Filling

2 cups diced round steak	4 cups diced potatoes
1 cup diced onion	½ of a medium rutabaga, diced
½ cup ground beef suet	1 teaspoon salt
dash pepper	2 tablespoons dried parsley

Mix filling ingredients in a large bowl until well blended. Roll the dough out on a floured board, one quarter at a time, and trace with a large dinner plate to get a circle 10 inches across. Mound a generous scoop of filling in center of circle and fold one side over to match edges, making a half-moon shape. Crimp edges to seal in the filling, prick top of crust and bake on a cookie sheet at 400 degrees until crust is golden brown, about 45 minutes.

MINER·HEATING·PASTY   MINER·HEATING·PASTY   MINER·HEATING·PASTY

Those Great Lakes!

The Great Lakes (Michigan, Ontario, Superior, Erie and Huron) are truly spectacular. The largest group of freshwater lakes in the world, they cover almost 95,000 square miles altogether and contain 6 quadrillion gallons of water! Formed 10,000 years ago by glaciers, the Great Lakes have played an important part in every aspect of Michigan, past and present.

The abundant fish in the lakes (salmon, lake trout, brown trout, whitefish, bass and many others) were a direct source of food for early inhabitants as well as providing a living for commercial fishermen today. There are also thousands of sports fishermen who come to the lakes every year, adding to the economy of the Great Lakes region. But pollution has become a serious threat to the Great Lakes in recent years, and we must work now to control this problem if we're going to continue to enjoy one of our greatest natural resources. The three main pollutants are sewage, detergents, and pesticide run-off from farms.

As a source of water travel, the Great Lakes have no rival. In fact, we have the largest freshwater transportation network in the world. From the Indians and settlers of long ago to the giant shipping industry of today, the Great Lakes and rivers of our state have made it possible to transport trade goods from the Upper Peninsula to the East cheaply and efficiently. Due to three man-made canals (the Soo Locks, the Welland Canal, and the St. Lawrence Seaway), it's possible to travel by boat from Lake Superior to the Atlantic Ocean! For example, to go to the Atlantic you would sail from Lake Superior through the Soo Locks into Lake Huron; from Lake Huron through the St. Clair River to Lake Erie; from Lake Erie up through the Welland Canal at Niagara Falls, New York, to the St. Lawrence Seaway and out to the ocean.

OTHER FACTS:

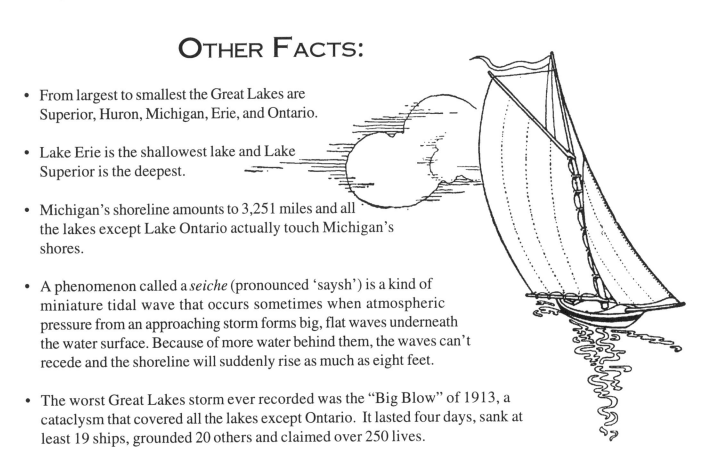

- From largest to smallest the Great Lakes are Superior, Huron, Michigan, Erie, and Ontario.

- Lake Erie is the shallowest lake and Lake Superior is the deepest.

- Michigan's shoreline amounts to 3,251 miles and all the lakes except Lake Ontario actually touch Michigan's shores.

- A phenomenon called a *seiche* (pronounced 'saysh') is a kind of miniature tidal wave that occurs sometimes when atmospheric pressure from an approaching storm forms big, flat waves underneath the water surface. Because of more water behind them, the waves can't recede and the shoreline will suddenly rise as much as eight feet.

- The worst Great Lakes storm ever recorded was the "Big Blow" of 1913, a cataclysm that covered all the lakes except Ontario. It lasted four days, sank at least 19 ships, grounded 20 others and claimed over 250 lives.

I Never Will Sail

Verse

Bm | A | Bm | A | Bm

I've been a sail- or all my life, ev-er since I was a ba- by, my

Bm | A | Bm | A | Bm

ma- ma cried when I was two 'cause I ran a- way to join the Na- vy. I

G | D | Em | F#

packed my dia- pers in a bag and I kissed her on the cheek. I

Bm | A | Bm | E | F# | Bm | F#

sailed a- way in the kit- chen sink and said I'd write next week! Oh,

Chorus

Bm | F#

ho, ho, ho, (ho, ho, ho) hee, hee, hee, (hee, hee, hee) I

Bm | F# | Bm | E | G | A | Bm

nev-er will sail on those Great Lakes for that'd be the end of me!

First I sailed the South Seas with their monsters by the dozens
I got in a fight with a giant squid and fifteen of his cousins
But they didn't scare me one little bit; I tied 'em in a bunch
And I fried 'em up with cheddar cheese, and I ate 'em for my lunch! oh!
Chorus

Then I sailed the ocean that they call Atlantic
Where a pirate with just one glass eye had all the folks there frantic
I said I'd make him toe the line, and it wasn't very hard
I warned him if he didn't behave, I'd take his library card! oh!
Chorus

Then I went to Michigan to sail that famous lake
And still I wasn't nervous when the boat began to shake
Then the sky grew dark until I couldn't see my First Mate Tommy
And I grabbed my favorite Teddy Bear and said, "I want my Mommy!"
Chorus

Chicora

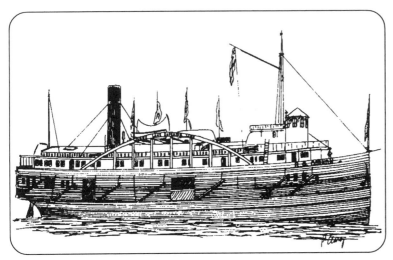

Stories of shipwrecks on the Great Lakes abound and, for many of them, the details of the mishaps are secrets that lie deep in the cold lake waters. We can only wonder what happened to the ships that never reached their destinations and what became of the men that sailed on them. While touring a historical home in our mid-Michigan community of St. Johns, however, we recently stumbled on information that brings a little insight into the last moments of the *Chicora*, a well-publicized wreck in the late 1800s.

The current homeowners brought out a box of faded photographs and scraps of paper that had been in the house for many years, detailing the attempts of one of the victims of the shipwreck to leave a message for his family. Intrigued by the mysterious connection between our town and the famous wreck, we searched through historical archives for accounts of the disaster, hoping to find the link between Lake Michigan and this rural community. None of the reports mention the message, but we did find that the owner of the house was the sister of the widowed woman and can only assume that the letters were kept in the family for personal reasons.

The morning of January 21, 1895, was warm, almost balmy; a welcome break in the hard winter weather typical in Great Lakes towns. In Milwaukee, Wisconsin, the *Chicora*, a stout, well-built passenger and freight ship of the Graham and Morton Line, was getting ready to sail across Lake Michigan to the twin ports of Benton Harbor and St. Joseph, Michigan. There was only one passenger that day, Mr. Joseph Pearl, who was going to Michigan to seek medical advice. The remaining personnel consisted of 25 crew members including the captain, Edward Stines, the chief engineer, Robert McClure of Detroit, and Captain Stines' son, Bennie, who had agreed to fill in for a crew member.

In St. Joseph, John Graham, one of the owners of the *Chicora*, was up early. He saw the barometer was falling quickly and fearing violent weather, sent a wire to Milwaukee ordering the *Chicora* not to sail. Unfortunately, the *Chicora* was already three or four ship lengths out on the lake when the message came, and attempts to contact her failed. Within hours the mild, spring-like weather turned into a raging gale, and watchers on the Michigan side anxiously scanned the lake for signs of the vessel.

Hour after hour passed with no word from or about the overdue *Chicora*. Finally, a couple of days later the lighthouse keeper at South Haven, Charles Donoghue, spied pieces of wreckage several miles out from shore. Rescue teams quickly were dispatched to the area, hoping to somehow find signs of survivors among the ice. No men were found but many pieces of the wreck were towed back to shore where they were identified as belonging to the *Chicora*.

All hands were assumed lost and almost three months later, on April 14, 1895, a bottle was found washed up on the shore by South Haven. In the bottle was a note hastily scrawled by the chief engineer of the *Chicora*, Robert McClure, bidding farewell to his wife and five children as the ship was sinking. Parts of the note are difficult to make out, but to the best of our knowledge the chilling message reads:

All is lost could see land if not snowed and blowed—engine given out drifting to shore on ice Robert McClure Captain and first mate swept off we have had a bad time of it 10:15 o'clock goodby.

For months after the wreck of the *Chicora* pieces of the ship washed up on the shores of Lake Michigan and years later a large part of Robert McClure's engineer's chair was found. The loss of her husband was certainly hard on Mrs. McClure, but we like to think she got some comfort from knowing he did his best to tell her good-bye.

Every ship on the Great Lakes carries a logo or insignia of its company on the stack so it can be identified from shore. Here are some of the hundreds of stack vessel emblems used by various Great Lakes shipping companies.

Logging

The bunkhouse or bunk shanty was home all winter for the lumberjacks, but it wasn't much to brag about. The building was made of logs with the spaces in between chinked with clay to keep out the cold. The only heat came from a potbellied stove in the middle of the room stoked with logs. Early bunkhouses didn't even have a stove or a wooden floor. A space was left in the middle of the dirt floor for a pile of logs four to five feet long, and that was the central heating system!

The bunkhouse was about 60' x 30' with sleeping bunks along each wall. The lower bunk was about one foot off the floor, the next one three feet above that. The slats of the bunks were poles or pieces of logs laid crosswise on the frame. The "mattress" on top of the poles consisted of cedar or hemlock boughs covered with a layer of hay. A grain sack filled with more hay served as a pillow, and a not-very-clean blanket topped it off. The lumberjacks were so worn out by the end of the day that they didn't really mind their surroundings that much. Before going to bed they would hang up wet socks, pants, and boots to dry overnight.

Sunday was a day for resting, playing cards, writing letters, mending clothes and "boiling up." A huge pot of water was brought to a boil on the stove and in it was tossed lye, yellow soap, and a good-sized plug of Peerless Chewing Tobacco. Into this magic concoction went lice-infested clothing, guaranteed to come out clean!

The hammered dulcimer (also called the Michigan dulcimer) supplied some of the music for Saturday night dances. Because there were no women in camp, some of the men would tie a red bandana around one arm and be the "ladies" for the dance.

Michigan was sparsely populated until the 1840s when vast tracts of timber were discovered here, especially the white pine which was in great demand in the East. Men began coming to Michigan by the trainloads (as many as 2,000 a day) to work in the lumber camps. In the 60-year period considered the Logging Era (1840-1900), over 161 billion board feet of pine were produced from our forests as well as another 50 billion board feet from other woods. The lumbermen led a hard and unglamorous life, beginning their workday before dawn and often going to bed before eight o'clock! The men needed big, starchy meals to keep them working in the cold northern woods, and a typical breakfast might consist of fried potatoes, sowbelly, pickled beef, navy beans, sourdough pancakes with molasses or gravy, cookies the size of stovelids, and pots of strong coffee and tea. After a rough six-day work week the lumberjacks were ready to loosen up on Saturday night and indulge in a little entertainment. The man who could play an instrument, sing a song, or tell a good story was a real asset to the lumber camp, and a rich array of lumberjack lore was left in Michigan long after the Logging Era was over.

Each lumber camp had an identifying symbol or mark that was stamped onto the log ends to prevent theft by other owners, much as cattle rustling was discouraged in the West by the practice of branding. The log marks were registered in the courthouse of the county where the camps were located. In one year alone over 1,100 log marks were registered on one river!

The lumberjacks or "shanty boys" were the men who cut the trees down in winter, lopped off branches, cut the logs to size and stacked them in piles. The rivermen or "riverhogs" were the men who floated the logs down the river to the sawmills. Some of the work involved in the river drive was very dangerous, and there were men who only came to the lumber camp in the spring to work as riverhogs. When one log would get stuck sideways in the river all the others would pile up behind it causing a "logjam." One brave man would walk out in the middle of the pile and free the "key log" (the one in the way) and then leap back to shore before the logs started moving again.

Here is a list of some terms used in the lumber camps:

SHANTY BOY—lumberjack, logger, or woodsman. The man who worked in the lumber camp cutting trees and getting them ready for the sawmill.

CROSS-CUT—a big curved saw with handles at each end so two men could saw logs together.

ROAD-MONKEY—the man who built the roads in the lumber camp.

BIG WHEEL—a flat-bedded wagon with huge wheels used for hauling logs out of the woods.

LOOKER—a man sent into the woods to find good timber for a landowner. Also called a timber cruiser.

SCALER—the man who measured the board feet of lumber in each log.

CHEAT STICK—the scale used by the scaler; similar to a yardstick.

DEACON—the man in camp who entertained by singing songs and telling stories.

TEAMSTER—the man who drove the teams of horses and oxen in camp.

COOKEE—the cook's helper. He peeled potatoes, hauled wood, drew water, lit fires and did anything else the cook needed to have done.

GABRIEL—a very long horn (sometimes 8 feet) made of tin that the Cookee blew to call the men to meals.

RIVERHOGS—the men who drove the logs from the woods to the booming ground at the sawmill. Also called riverdrivers, riverjacks, and riverpigs.

WANIGAN—a camp store and kitchen built on a raft that floated behind the rivermen during the spring drive.

VALLEY BOYS—loggers from the Saginaw Valley who had a reputation for being rougher and tougher than any other lumberjacks.

ichigan produces more navy beans (also called Michigan beans) than any other state in the country. In fact, we harvest almost 500 million pounds of beans a year! The lumber camps in Michigan served beans at dinner much too often for some of the men, and the song on the next page expresses the way most of them felt about it. However, we think this combination of beans and sausage is unbeatable.

BEAN AND SAUSAGE SOUP

1¼ cups Michigan beans
4 tablespoons butter
2 cups finely chopped onions
2 carrots, finely chopped
3 cloves garlic, minced
1 teaspoon dried parsley
1 teaspoon thyme

1 bay leaf
4 cups chicken stock
1 sweet green pepper
1 sweet red pepper
½ pound kielbasa or knockwurst
2 tablespoons olive oil

Soak beans overnight in water to cover. (Or bring beans to a boil for one minute, turn off heat and let sit, covered, for one hour.) Drain beans after softened and set aside. In large, heavy pot melt butter; add onions, carrots and garlic and cook over low heat until tender, about 25 minutes. Add parsley, thyme, bay leaf, chicken stock, and beans. Bring mixture to a boil; then reduce heat and simmer, partially covered, until the beans are tender, about one hour. Remove bay leaf and, if desired, put beans in food mill or food processor and process until smooth, returning to pot. Core and chop green and red peppers and sauté in olive oil until crisp tender. Drain and add to soup pot. Slice sausage, removing skin if necessary, and add to soup. Heat soup through, season to taste with salt and pepper.

he lumberjacks in Michigan used to eat molasses cookies the size of stove lids! (A stove lid, in case you didn't know, is a circle about 8 inches across.) We think these molasses cookies are some of the best we've ever tasted. You can try making them as big as a dinner plate if you want, but you'll have to share! Have your mom help you experiment with the size of dough balls you'll need for giant cookies.

BUNYAN MOLASSES COOKIES

1 cup sugar
¾ cup margarine
4 tablespoons molasses
1 egg
2 cups flour

1 teaspoon ginger
2½ teaspoons baking soda
¼ teaspoon salt
1 teaspoon cinnamon (or more)

With an electric mixer cream the sugar and margarine until well blended. Then beat in the molasses and egg. In a medium-sized bowl stir the remaining ingredients together; then add to the sugar mixture. Let the dough chill in the refrigerator for about three hours until it's not sticky anymore. (This might be a good time to pick up your toys!) When dough is chilled, pre-heat the oven to 375 degrees and lightly grease a cookie sheet. Break off pieces of dough and roll them into the size of a walnut. Roll the pieces in sugar and place them on the cookie sheet about six inches apart; don't press them down. Bake for about 10 minutes, being careful not to overbake.

Louie Sands and Jim McGee

Public domain
Usually sung a cappella to "O Tannenbaum"

Who feeds us beans? who feeds us tea? Lou-ie Sands and Jim Mc-Gee! Who thinks that meat's a lux-u-ry? Lou-ie Sands and Jim Mc-Gee! Who makes the big trees fall ker-splash and hit the ground an aw-ful smash and for the logs who gets the cash? Lou-ie Sands and Jim Mc-Gee. Who Jim Mc-Gee.

Who feeds us beans until we're blue? Louie Sands and Jim McGee
Who thinks that nothing else will do? Louie Sands and Jim McGee
Who feeds us beans three times a day
And gives us very little pay?
Who feeds us beans, again I say? Louie Sands and Jim McGee!

Who feeds us beans each blessed day? Louie Sands and Jim McGee
Who'll feed us beans 'til Judgment Day? Louie Sands and Jim McGee
And when that judgment's past and we
Know just where we're going to be
Who'll feed us beans through Eternity? Louie Sands and Jim McGee!

KIDNEY BEANS · LIMA BEANS · MUNG BEANS · NAVY BEANS · PINTO BEANS · BLACK BEANS

Roll Loggers Roll

We came from the East and we came in a line— Roll, log- gers, roll, to the

Sag-i-naw Val-ley to cut the White Pi-ne, Roll, you log- gers, roll We were

swam-pers and ri-ver hogs, shan-ty boys, too, Roll, log- gers, roll, we

all were a part of the whole log-ging crew, Roll, you log- gers, roll.

Roll, (clap) roll, (clap) roll, you log- gers, roll. For roll.

For breakfast there was pancakes with gravy and beans—roll loggers, roll
Taters and sowbelly, coffee and tea—roll you loggers, roll
Then off to the woods in the dark we would go—roll loggers, roll
To work all day long in the cold and the snow—roll you loggers, roll
Roll! (clap) Roll! (clap) Roll, you loggers, roll!

Sometimes we'd dress up and go into town—roll loggers, roll
To flirt with the girls and to drink cider down—roll you loggers, roll
The winters were long and the lice they did bite—roll loggers, roll
But it's not a bad life and we liked it all right—roll you loggers, roll
Roll! (clap) Roll! (clap) Roll, you loggers, roll!

The Round River Drive

aul Bunyan was a giant lumberjack who used to log in the North woods many years ago, sometimes out West and sometimes in Michigan. Paul had a pet, a giant blue ox, named Babe.

Sometimes Paul had strange adventures in the woods, and the one he liked to tell about most was the tale of the Round River Drive. It seems as though it went like this:

Paul and his lumberjacks had set up camp in a new spot one fall, where they worked hard all that winter, felling trees and stacking 'em by the river. Finally it got to be spring, and they were all looking forward to the river drive. (You remember—that's when all the logs are floated down the river to the sawmill.) Well, Paul and the boys piled those logs on the river and got their raft all rigged up and ready to go. Before they left, though, Paul thought he'd better do a little spring cleaning; so he got a big kettle full of boiling water, threw in some yellow soap and washed out his winter underwear—his bright red underwear—the long-john kind that's all one piece from the neck to the ankles. Paul hoisted his underwear up on the flagpole so it'd be nice and dry by the time they got back from the log drive and he could pack it away with his other winter duds.

One bright morning they took off and Paul and his buddies floated along behind those logs for about a week, making small talk and lookin' at the scenery when one day in the distance they noticed a puff of smoke above the trees.

"Hmmmm! Must be another lumber camp!" said Paul. "I thought we were the only ones around here. Wonder who it could be?"

Well, the polite thing would've been to stop and visit, but time was getting on, so they just nodded and waved as they drifted by.

"Y'know," said Joe Murphy, "that feller that waved back looked an awful lot like Cream Puff Fatty, our cook. And that shed over there looks big enough for Babe. And say! Somebody else has his bright red underwear hangin' on the flagpole, just like you, Paul."

Well, Paul thought this was a strange kind of coincidence, but pretty soon he forgot about it, being so busy as he was.

About a week later, Paul and the boys came around a bend in the river and, surprise! There was another camp like theirs with a cook like Cream Puff Fatty, a huge barn like Babe's and there, blowing in the breeze was a pair of bright red underwear, just like Paul's!

This time Paul didn't take it so lightly, and even though he waved at the cook, he was muttering under his breath about how he'd have to look into this when he got back from the sawmill.

It was the third time they came around a bend and saw a camp like theirs, with a cook just like theirs, and a big pair of bright red underwear just like Paul's that they all decided to go see who owned this camp and maybe find out who owned the other two. I mean, the woods were pretty big, but loggers need their cuttin' room.

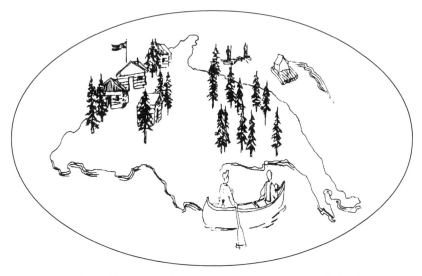

So Paul and the boys pulled their raft over to the river bank and climbed out. Paul started stomping up to the cookhouse when the door flew open and who should step out but . . .Cream Puff Fatty himself!

Paul stared at Cream Puff, astonished.

The rotund cook said, "Y'know, we've been watchin' you boys float by the camp about every week or so, and we was wonderin' where you were goin'."

"You mean it's you we've been wavin' at? And it's Babe's barn we've been seeing? And dangling up there on the flagpole is my own bright red underwear?"

"Well sure," answered Cream Puff. "Whose else would it be?"

About then Paul got an idea in his head, and he knew right away what had been going on. The spot they had picked for their camp was on the famous Round River! The Round River was a perfect circle, and there was no way out—and no sawmill, either—and they'd just been going around and around, again and again and again.

Now you'd think Paul and the boys would've been pretty mad about wasting all that time going nowhere, but instead they just had a big Sourdough Flapjack Reunion Dinner with their camp mates, and they all laughed about that adventure, long and hard. They figured this story would be good for many a long winter.

CELERY CANOE AND SALMON, TOO

For a nice change from tuna salad, try using salmon, adding or subtracting your favorite condiments: dill pickle relish, mustard, black olives, artichoke hearts, etc. Our kids loved these little hors d'oeurves.

1 small can salmon, skin and bones removed
2 to 3 tablespoons mayonnaise
2 tablespoons chopped olives
1 teaspoon minced onion

Flake salmon into a medium-sized bowl and add other ingredients, mixing well. Spread on whole wheat crackers (rafts) or into cleaned celery stalks (canoes) and eat!

Rivers

Michigan's rivers, over 36,000 miles worth, still bear the names of their "discoverers" from many years ago, which makes for an interesting combination of French, Indian and English names. This song pairs some of those names with an old fiddle tune.

There's the Ti-ta ba-wa-see and the Shi-a-wa-see, too, the bold Red Ce-dar and the Ka-la-ma- zoo, and the Big Two- Heart-ed and the Lit-tle Man- i-stee; the Hur-ri-cane Ri-ver and St. Paul's Creek.

Chorus

Wa- ter, wa- ter all a- round- creeks and streams for miles a- bound, blue and roll- ing, calm and green- Mi-chi-gan's ri-vers run cold and clean. There's the cold and clean.

There's the Pigeon River and the Pere Marquette
The Ontonagon and the sweet little Betsie
River Raisin and the Salt and the Cass
The Maple River and the Looking Glass
Chorus

There's the Rifle River and the Pine and the Ford
The Escanaba and the Black and the Boardman
Devil's River and the old Paw Paw
The Thornapple River and the Chippewa
Chorus

There's the St. Marys River and the Belle and the Flint
Tahquamenon River and the Flat and the Clinton
Saginaw River and the long Au Gres
The Paint and the Rabbit and the Thunder Bay
Chorus

There's the Sturgeon River and the Chocolay
The Sand and the Silver and the Eagle and the Slate
The Yellow Dog River and the Misery
The Laughing Whitefish and the Michigamme
Chorus

Paul Bunyan for Little Loggers

Here is our three-in-one doll. The pattern on this page can be used to make all three of our doll projects: Crazy-Leg-Logger and Bunyan Boy (found on page 32), and the paper doll (described here). We recommend photocopying these pages. The pattern should be used to cut the paper doll out of poster board. The doll's wardrobe on the next page may be photocopied, colored, and cut out. Additional outfits are easily designed by tracing the doll onto a clean sheet of paper and adding tabs.

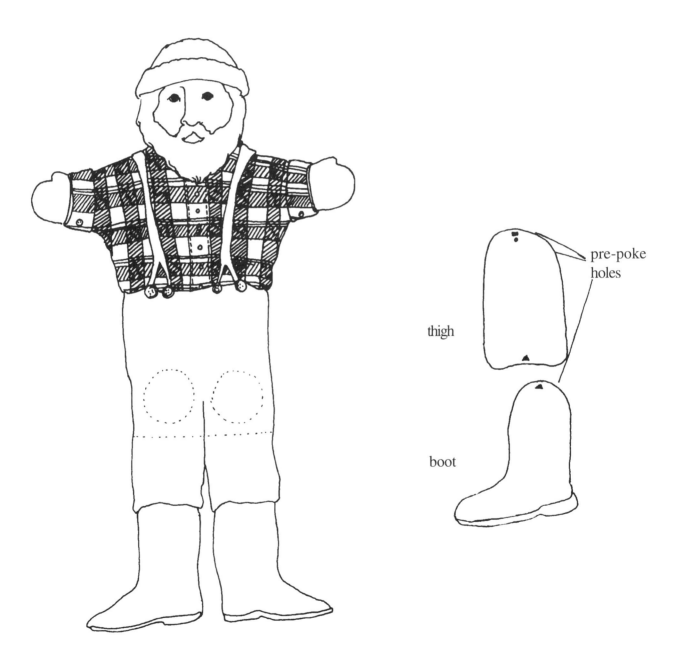

pre-poke holes

thigh

boot

On the next page is Paul's wardrobe from the inside out. Your doll can dress for everything from a "river hog" with his special cork boots and fancy sash, to the cook, the favorite person in camp! We've even included the very important long-john underwear on the following page to snuggle in bed with at the end of a busy day.

Bunyan Boy

When held from the top and pulled by the string below, our Bunyan Boy kicks up his heels, and dances the Lumberjack's Stomp. This is our version of an old Appalachian wooden folk toy whose linkage of strings on the back side allows for his double-jointed flexibility. Even these old folk toys were based on the old, pasteboard dolls called "pantins" that were popular in France during the 1700s.

By using the master copy on the previous page as the pattern, you then cut it out of poster board. Cut out all the pieces and then pre-poke holes with a large needle. If cutting poster board is too difficult for your little one, assembling could be a fun helper's project. Color your pieces now before assembling. Using a needle and thread, attach the boot to the thigh. Repeat with second leg. Now connect the two legs by stringing them together at the matching dots found on the thighs. Tie a small piece of thread midway between the two thighs. This will be the pull-string. Now all that is left is to attach both legs to the main body at the squares at the top of the thighs.

Points to remember:
1) Keep your stitches loose when attaching body parts. This will avoid stiff joints.
2) To end each stitch, simply tie a small knot on the back side of the puppet.

The Finger Puppet

Our Crazy-Legs-Logger is so light on his feet! Cut and color, then your puppet is ready for a long day's work, a Saturday night dance, or a run to the cook's cabin for a hearty helping of bean soup.

Photocopy the master copy from the preceding page as a pattern and then cut out your puppet from some poster board. Cut out the circles so that your fingers will become the puppet's legs. (Younger children may need assistance at this point.) Color your puppet. Now using your first and second fingers as legs, your puppet will be ready to run and play.

Little Loggers

A simple fingerplay for the younger set. Even small children can understand the need to be careful with our resources.

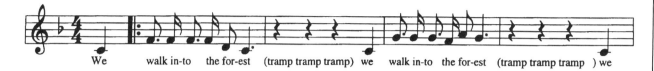

We walk in-to the for-est (tramp tramp tramp) we walk in-to the for-est (tramp tramp tramp) we

walk in-to the for-est (tramp tramp tramp) and find our-selves a tree.

1. **Fine**

We tree.

We walk into the forest—tramp, tramp, tramp
(pat hands on knees)
repeat twice
And find ourselves a tree

We swing our axe—whoosh, whoosh, whoosh
(swing arms back and forth)
repeat twice
And start to cut it down

Then we cut that tree—chop, chop, chop
(chopping motion)
repeat twice
'Til it's laying on the ground

Then we float it down the river—easy, boys!
(flowing motion with hands)
repeat twice
To the sawmill in the town

Then we saw it into boards—bzz, bzz, bzz
(circular sawing motions)
repeat twice
That are wide and flat and long

Then we plant another seed—pat, pat, pat
(patting motion)
repeat twice
To grow another tree

Pretzel Log Cabin

For a simple, edible house try making this pretzel log cabin. Little Loggers may need some help. All you need is:

> about 40 small pretzels
> ½ cup powdered sugar
> ¼ teaspoon water

In a small bowl, blend the sugar and water until you have a thick, smooth paste. This is the mortar (cement) that will hold your 'logs' together. Working on a large piece of waxed paper will help contain the mess.

To construct the cabin, you'll make three basic sections separately, connecting them together when they're dry.

For the walls, lay two pretzels (one pretzel length apart) on the waxed paper. For the opposite walls, dip each end of two more pretzels in the sugar cement and lay them across the two logs so you have a square. (Just like using Lincoln Logs!) Continue to build the walls alternating sides until the cabin is about 2 inches high. Set it gently aside to dry.

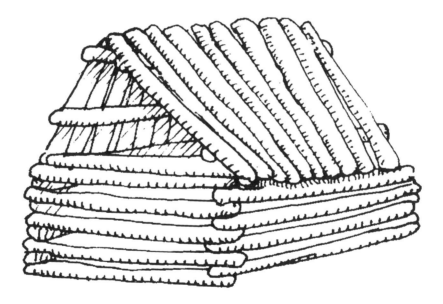

To build the roof, dip the whole length of two pretzels in the sugar cement and lay them on the waxed paper (sugared sides up) two inches apart. These will be the braces for one side of the roof. Lay pretzel logs across the cement, close together, leaving about 3/4 inch uncovered at one end. Repeat this procedure for the other side of the roof. Allow all sections to dry completely, about 30 minutes.

To complete the assembly, prop up the roof sides on the cabin base with the uncovered ends hanging down. Cement the pieces in place with sugar paste if necessary.

Henny and Benny Bunyan

"TAKING A BITE OUT OF MICHIGAN"

Just about everybody knows that Paul Bunyan was a giant lumberjack who lived and worked in the Michigan woods a long time ago. What might come as a surprise to some folks is that there are still Bunyans living in the Upper Peninsula, around the town of Christmas. (Yes, Virginia, there is a Christmas, Michigan.)

Henny and Benny Bunyan are brothers. Paul Bunyan was a distant cousin on their mother's side (twice removed): and although Paul was a very big person, Henny and Benny are just regular-sized guys.

Benny is the older brother. He's the one who usually keeps things organized, remembers to comb his hair, and doesn't leave the radio on when he's not listening to it. Benny wants to be a dentist or to make furniture when he grows up.

Henny, on the other hand, seems to have a hard time keeping his shoes tied, loses his lunch box a lot and his library books are always overdue. Henny is a dreamer and when he grows up he wants to be in show business; in fact, he thinks being a stand-up comic would be about the best job in the world. Henny has been practicing his jokes and working on his style while making a lot of appearances in the Pasty Belt.

Last summer Henny and Benny decided they would take a vacation trip around Michigan eating as much delicious food from our state as they could. (If you'd like to sample some of the tasty things they ate, turn to the next two pages for the recipes.) Before leaving Christmas, Benny stopped at the local grocery store and bought some **Thimbleberry Leather**. Henny asked his brother if he was going to make a belt or something.

"Naw," said Benny. "This is made out of dried fruit. We can carry it with us and if we get hungry we just tear off a piece and eat it. It's pretty good!"

By the time they got to St. Ignace, the boys were looking for someplace to eat lunch. They found a small fish shop and sat down to a heaping platter of **Deep Fried Lemon Smelt** and coleslaw. They ate until they were full and then wandered around the shop looking at the many kinds of fish on display.

After crossing the Mackinac Bridge, Henny and Benny decided to go to Traverse City and join in the Cherry Festival fun. The Traverse City area grows more sour cherries than any other area in the country. All the cherries looked so good that they ate four **Cherry Tarts** apiece! (Well, they were small tarts, honest!)

The next stop on the trip was in Harrison which is just about in the middle of the mitten. They spent many hours looking for morel mushrooms. They went with a guide, of course, who helped them tell the difference between mushrooms that are good to eat and those that could make them sick.

"I guess," said Henny, "the 'morel' of the story is that you better know what you are doing when it comes to mushrooms!"

That night they sat down to a supper of **Butter-Sautéed Morels**. Mmmmm.

The next morning the boys got up early and headed for Port Huron on the eastern side of the state. They discovered that the area grows lots and lots of potatoes so for breakfast they had sausages and **Potato Cheese Pancakes**.

Believe it or not, they decided the best thing to do after breakfast is to eat dessert (I hope they brought their toothbrushes!) so they headed for St. Johns where they had a big dish of **Kick-the-Can Ice Cream** with **Fudge Mint Sauce**. St. Johns grows a lot of the mint used in this country.

The last stop on their vacation took Henny and Benny to Detroit where they spent the day seeing the sights and riding on the People Mover. Oddly enough, though, they weren't hungry anymore. In fact, Henny had a bit of a stomachache, so they bought a big bottle of Vernor's Ginger Ale and two straws and headed back home.

Henny and Benny's Recipes

THIMBLEBERRY LEATHER

Very ripe thimbleberries, raspberries, or other ripe fruit

Gently wash berries and remove stems. Puree in blender. Stretch a piece of plastic wrap tightly over a cookie sheet, taping it in place. Spread pureed fruit as thinly as possible over plastic wrap and dry in a very low oven. (The pilot light in a gas oven should be sufficient.) Allow fruit to dry for about two days or until all moisture is evaporated. The leather can be peeled off the plastic to be eaten or it may be stored by rolling it in the plastic and keeping it in an airtight container.

DEEP-FRIED LEMON SMELT

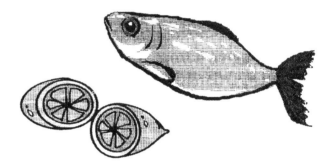

2 pounds pan-dressed smelt
juice of 2 lemons
2 cups white cornmeal
2 eggs, beaten
¼ cup milk
pinch black pepper
corn oil

In glass or stainless steel pan, marinate smelt in lemon juice about 20 minutes, tossing occasionally. Place cornmeal in flat dish. Combine eggs, milk, and pepper in medium bowl, beat until well mixed. In heavy skillet, heat enough corn oil to cover pan to a depth of one inch. Dip smelt in cornmeal, then in egg mixture and again in cornmeal. Fry fish until lightly browned on both sides. Drain. Serve with lemon.

SAUTEED MOREL MUSHROOMS

Morels (or store-bought mushrooms)
Butter

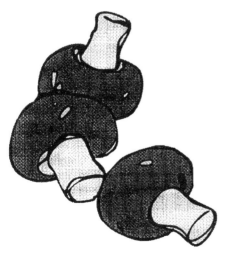

Wipe the morels with a damp paper towel. Don't soak them in water. Cut off stems and slice the caps in half lengthwise. Melt a generous amount of butter in a frying pan, put in enough mushrooms to cover bottom of pan, and salt, lightly. Saute about five minutes on each side and serve immediately.

EASY CHERRY TARTS

small (21 oz.) can cherry pie filling
1 stick pie crust mix (or recipe for 9" pie crust)

Prepare pie crust according to package directions. Roll crust out on a floured board to 1/8 inch thickness. Cut rounds about 4 inches across (you can use a saucer as a guide) and insert them carefully into muffin tins. Spoon cherry filling to the top of each crust and bake at 425 degrees for about 15-20 minutes or until crust is golden brown. Makes 4 to 6 tarts.

POTATO-CHEESE PANCAKES

4 medium potatoes, peeled and shredded
1 cup shredded Cheddar or Swiss cheese
¼ cup chopped onion
3 eggs
2 tbsp. flour
1 tsp. salt
1/8 tsp. black pepper

In large bowl mix potatoes, cheese, onion, eggs, flour, salt, and pepper. In large skillet heat enough cooking oil to coat bottom. Drop scoops (about ¼ cup each) of batter in pan, spreading evenly. Cook both sides over medium-high heat until golden brown. Drain on paper towels. Serve alone or with applesauce.

KICK-THE-CAN ICE CREAM

1 cup heavy cream
1 cup milk
1 beaten egg
1/3 to 1/2 cup sugar
1 tsp. vanilla
crushed ice (about 20 cups)
1½ cups rock or kosher salt

In a small coffee can (12-ounce or one-pound) with tight plastic lid, mix together cream, milk, beaten egg, sugar, and vanilla. In large (2 or 3 pound) coffee can, layer some of the crushed ice and salt on bottom. Place smaller filled can on top and pack half the ice and salt in space between cans and on top. Cover large can and kick (or roll) back and forth for 10 minutes. Drain melted ice out of large can, repack with remaining ice and salt and roll another 5 or 10 minutes. Remove small can and serve immediately or place in freezer.

FUDGE MINT SAUCE

1 cup sugar
¾ cup water
½ cup butter
¼ cup light corn syrup

1 pkg. (12 oz) chocolate chips
¼ cup creme de menthe or
1 tsp. peppermint extract

ꟿn medium saucepan combine sugar, water, butter (cut into small pieces) and corn syrup. Cook over medium heat, stirring constantly, until mixture comes to a full boil, about 5 to 8 minutes. Boil 3 minutes. Remove from heat and immediately add the chocolate chips, beating with a wire whisk until mixture is smooth and chocolate is melted. Stir in extract. Cool to lukewarm and pour into jars to store. Will keep up to 2 months in the refrigerator or 6 months in the freezer.

Spoon Sandwich

Once in a great while you may find yourself with nothing to do. You could take out the garbage, I suppose, or scrub the bathtub. But if those things don't seem to fill the bill, maybe you'd like to learn to play the spoons! Here's how . . .

Start by making a spoon sandwich using two teaspoons (or bigger spoons if your hands are big) and these two fingers. Your fingers are the baloney. Hold one spoon, bowl end up, between your thumb and baloney fingers.

The next spoon you slide on top of those two fingers (like the top piece of bread) so the bowls of the spoons are facing each other. Curl your ring and pinky fingers over the spoon handles to keep them in place.

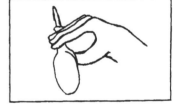

Now (very important) turn your hand so the spoon that was on top is on the bottom. If your thumb is facing up and your fingernails are facing you, you're holding them right. It takes a little practice to know how this should feel. Don't be afraid to adjust the spoon handles as needed. The bowls should not be touching each other.

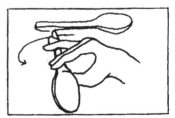

Now comes the fun part. Gently tap the spoons on your knee. As the bowls bump into each other, you'll get a clacking sound. Hold your other hand over the spoons to tap them back down as they come up. They clack again, and now you have two sounds!

When you've mastered this part, you can learn another trick that will really leave your audience breathless. Briefly hold the thumb and middle finger of your nonspoon hand together under the spoons as they go up and down. Now you should hear a whole bunch of clacks, like the sound of a horse galloping. You've just become a one-man band. Look out Hollywood!

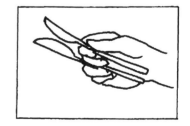

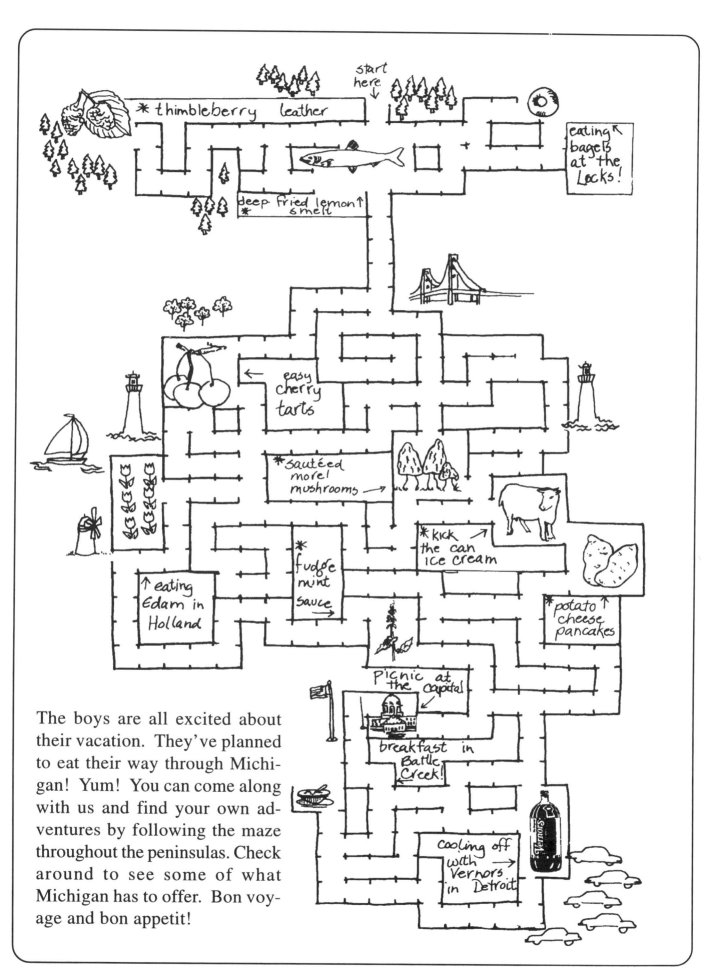

start here ↓

* thimbleberry leather

eating bagels at the Locks!

* deep fried lemon smelt ↑

← easy cherry tarts

* sautéed morel mushrooms →

* kick the can ice cream

* fudge mint sauce →

↑ eating Edam in Holland

* potato cheese pancakes ↑

Picnic at the capital →

breakfast in Battle Creek!

cooling off with Vernors in Detroit →

The boys are all excited about their vacation. They've planned to eat their way through Michigan! Yum! You can come along with us and find your own adventures by following the maze throughout the peninsulas. Check around to see some of what Michigan has to offer. Bon voyage and bon appetit!

Automobiles

Although most people think of Henry Ford as the pioneer of the auto, experiments with gasoline engines were going on in France, Belgium, and Germany for years before the summer of 1896 when Ford, Ransom Olds, and Charles B. King all displayed their versions of the gasoline-powered vehicle for the public. It was the introduction of the assembly line by Olds (with great improvements by Henry Ford) that really changed the face of transportation by making it possible to manufacture cars quickly, which made them affordable to the common man.

Wheels

This can be read as a poem or done as a "rap" style song, with everybody joining in on the chorus.
Snapping fingers and other rhythmic sounds make it more fun.

It used to be that to get to town
You had to keep a horse and a wagon around
And it took a long time to cover that ground
But there wasn't much a body could do

Then some guys named Olds and Ford got smart
And they put an engine on a four-wheeled cart
And it ran pretty good once they got it to start
With just a little nudge or two; and it went

Chorus
HONK HONK - BEEP BEEP - Bumpa-chicka, bumpa-chicka
HONK HONK - BEEP BEEP - Bumpa-chicka, bumpa-chicka
HONK HONK - BEEP BEEP - Bumpa-chicka, bumpa-chicka HONK HONK!!!

When that buggy came rumblin' down the street
A commotion started that couldn't be beat
Why, ladies fainted right off of their feet
They'd never seen such power

Dogs were barking and children ran
And down for a look came every man
And they gasped at the sight of this big tin can
Going twenty miles an hour; and it went

Chorus

Well, those horse and buggy days are past
And folks quit saying, "it'll never last"
And we have big factories to put 'em out fast
in every color and size

Now there's sporty cars with chrome on the side
And family cars with families inside
And fancy cars where the rich folks ride
From that first automotive surprise; and it went

Chorus

Michigan Gals

Based on "Buffalo Gals"

Chorus

Mich-i-gan gals, won't you come out to-night, come out to-night, come out to-night?

Mich-i-gan gals, won't you come out to-night and dance by the light of the moon?

Verse

We went down to Ka-la-ma-zoo where they do the Bu-ga-loo, the
To Three Ri-vers Kawe-did go, where we hoofed it, heel and toe, then

Two-step and the Tan-go, too, and we danced by the light of the moon. Then moon.
shuf-fled off to Buf-fa-lo, and we danced by the light of the moon.

Then we went up to Cadillac; we can't wait 'til we get back
To the Rooster Walk and the Turkey Track and we'll dance by the light of the moon
Then on we went to Charlevoix; clogging is what they enjoy
Every girl there grabbed a boy and they danced by the light of the moon

Chorus

Then we went up to Ishpeming where those folks know how to swing
With the Irish Jig and the Highland Fling and we danced by the light of the moon
Then we slid over to Marquette where we had the best time yet
We polka'd all night long, you bet! and we danced by the light of the moon

Chorus

Then in Bay City we did stop where we did the Bunny Hop
The Rhumba and the B.C. Bop and we danced by the light of the moon
At last we got to Lansing town just in time for the big Hoedown
We danced a Square and then a Round and we danced by the light of the moon

Chorus

Michigan Kids

Here's another fingerplay for youngsters.

We're from Mi-chi-gan, we are Num-ber One, we're from Mi-chi-gan, we are Num-ber One, we're
good kids, we're great kids, we are Mi-chi-gan kids!

We're from Michigan, we are Number One (hold up index finger)
We're from Michigan, we are Number One
We're good kids! (one arm punches air)
We're great kids! (other arm punches air)
We are Michigan kids (hands on hips)

We have two peninsulas (hold up index and middle fingers)
The upper and the lower (other hand indicates up and down)
We have two peninsulas, the upper and the lower
We're good kids! We're great kids! We are Michigan kids!

We have lots of shoreline (index, middle and ring fingers)
3,000 miles in all (other arm sweeps in an arc)
We have lots of shoreline, 3,000 miles in all
We're good kids! We're great kids! We are Michigan kids!

We have four big bridges (all four fingers up)
That go across the water (other arm forms bridge)
We have four big bridges that go across the water
We're good kids! We're great kids! We are Michigan kids!

We're from Michigan
We'll give you a hand (hold up "Mitten" hand)
We're from Michigan, we'll give you a hand
We're good kids! We're great kids! We are Michigan kids!

Singing and Signing

American Sign Language (ASL) is a nonvocal language used to communicate with persons who are deaf or hearing impaired. ASL uses both fingerspelling (signing the letters of the alphabet) and symbols that convey words or ideas and was developed from a similar system taught in France in the early 1800s. Different regions of the country have their own variations of sign language, and it's possible to tell where a person is from by their "accent" in sign. Even preschoolers can learn simple songs in sign.

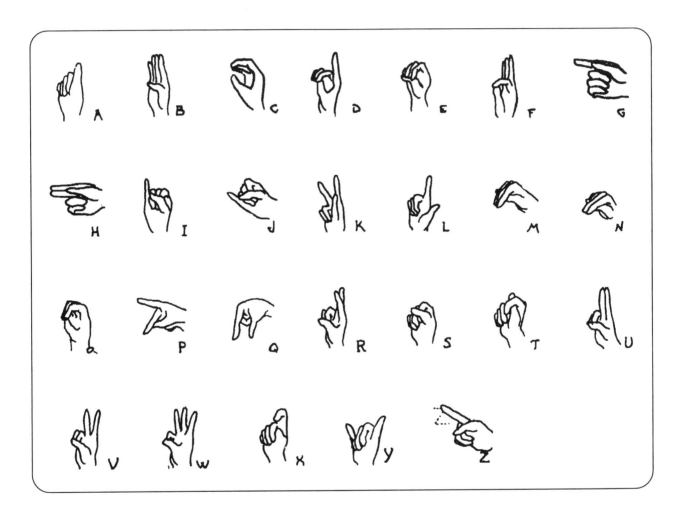

To tie up the song *Where I Live* (see next page) with a Michigan ending you can use the last four measures of the tune to sign M-I-C-H-I-G-A-N.

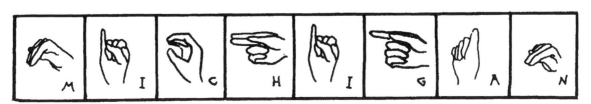

Where I Live

Where I live we have lots of trees
Where I live we have lots of cars
Where I live we have lots of snow
Where I live we have lots of friends

Michigan ABC

Based on "The Lumberjack's Alphabet"

Verse

A is for au-tos that we're fa-mous for B is blue-ber-ries we grow by the score,

C is for Cal-u-met's Cop-per Coun-try and D is De-troit that's our big-gest ci-ty. So

Chorus

mer-ry, so mer-ry, so mer-ry are we, we are from Mi-chi-gan and glad to be, sing

hi der-ry hey der-ry ho der-ry dum, if you need more rea-sons then we'll give you some!

E is for Erie, one of the Great Lakes
F is for Finns bringing skis and fish cakes
G is for Gerald Ford, once President, and
H is for Holland where the Dutch settlers went.

Chorus

I is for Iron Ore deep in the mines
J is our miles of White and Jack Pines
K is for Kelloggs, who gave us corn flakes, and
L is for Leelanau, loggers and lakes

Chorus

M is for Mackinac Island nearby
N is the Northern Lights filling the sky
O is for Ojibwa and Oldsmobile, and
P is for pasties, a wonderful meal!

Chorus

Q is for Quincy, a big copper mine
R is the Robin, our state bird so fine
S is for Soo Locks that ships can pass
    through, and
T is for Tigers, Tahquamenon, too.

Chorus

U is U.P. with spectacular views
V is for voyageurs in their canoes
W is Water, it's plenty we've got, and
X marks the fabulous Mystery Spot!

Chorus

Y is the city of Ypsilanti
Z is for Zeeland and the end of this spree
Our time is all up and we're through with
    this song
But to think up more verses it won't take
    you long

Last Chorus
Sing hi derry, hey derry, ho derry dum
If you need more reasons then you think
    of some!

Michigan Waltz

Verse

Spring in this coun- try starts win- dy and gray 'til the
sun set- tles in chas- ing win- ter a- way the
mourn- ing dove calls as the leaves take their bow, you can
smell the dark earth turn- ing un- der the plow; and the
days they grow long- er, our feet they go bare as the
drone of the bees puts a spell in the air.

Chorus

Round and round go the sea-sons in Mi-chi-gan, round and round like a waltz on the floor.
Turn, swing, slide, step, back a-gain and al-ways we dance one more.

Summer's a symphony, a joyous crescendo
Of berries and sweet corn and grass in the meadow
The Great Lakes come crashing down onto the land
While the dunes lay like giants asleep in the sand
Night sounds ring out 'neath a waxed paper moon
'Til the harvest begins and it's over too soon
Chorus

Bittersweet Autumn brings frost in the morning
When the maple and sumac catch fire without warning
There's pumpkins and cider and smoke on the wind
And the wild geese say, "good-bye, we'll be back again."
Indian Summer puts on a good show
'Til a blast from the North brings a sky full of snow
Chorus

In the silence of Winter in trees beyond number
You can still hear faint echoes of long ago lumbermen
Dancing and laughing with songs all around
And the snow lays like sugar on city and town
Throw a log on the fire, the hard work is done
'Til the smelt fill the rivers and sap starts to run
Chorus

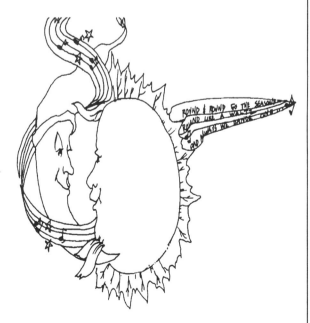

Other Books About Michigan

Beacons of Light: Lighthouses by Gail Gibbons

Ghost Ships of the Great Lakes by Dwight Boyer

Crooked Tree: Indian Legends of Northern Michigan by John C. Wright

Grandmother Moon Speaks by Simon Otto

Great Lakes & Great Ships: Illustrated History for Children by John Mitchell & Tom Woodruff

Great Lakes Shipwrecks & Survivals by William Ratigan

Hiawatha Legends by Henry R. Schoolcraft

Harps Upon the Willows: Johnston Family of the Old Northwest by Marjorie Cahn Brazer

In the Palm of the Mitten by Bernice Chappel

Indians of the Great Lakes: Illustrated History for Children by John Mitchell & Tom Wood

Joy of Signing by Lottie L. Rickehof

Maple Sugar Book by Helen and Scott Nearing

Memories of the Lakes by Dana Owen

Michigan Gold: Mining in the Upper Peninsula by Daniel R. Fountain

Michigan on Fire by Betty Sodders

Michigan: History of the Wolverine State by Willis F. Dunbar and George S. May

Michigan: Illustrated History for Children by John Mitchell & Tom Woodruff

Most Superior Land: Life in the Upper Peninsula of Michigan edited by Susan Newhof Pyle

Nishnawbe by Lynne Deur

Old Forts of the Great Lakes: Sentinels in the Wilderness by James P. Barry

Pictorial History of the Great Lakes by Harlan H. Hatcher and Erich Walker

Schooners in Peril: True and Exciting Stories About Tall Ships on the Great Lakes by James L. Donahue

Settling in Michigan by Lynne Deur

Ships of the Great Lakes: 300 Years of Navigation by James P. Barry

Steaming Through Smoke and Fire: True Stories of Shipwreck and Disaster on the Great Lakes: 1871 by James L. Donahue

Women Who Kept the Lights: Illustrated History of Female Lighthouse Keepers by Mary and J. Candace Clifford

Wrecks and Rescues of the Great Lakes by James P. Barry